HOW? WHO? WHAT? WHEN? WHERE? WHY?

Questions kids ask

ABOUT
ART AND ENTERTAINMENT

PUBLISHER	Joseph R. DeVarennes
PUBLICATION DIRECTOR	Kenneth H. Pearson
ADVISORS	Roger Aubin Robert Furlonger
EDITORIAL SUPERVISOR	Jocelyn Smyth
PRODUCTION MANAGER	Ernest Homewood

PRODUCTION ASSISTANTS

Martine Gingras Kathy Kishimoto
Catherine Gordon Peter Thomlison

CONTRIBUTORS

Alison Dickie Nancy Prasad
Bill Ivy Lois Rock
Jacqueline Kendel Merebeth Switzer
Anne Langdon Dave Taylor
Sheila Macdonald Alison Tharen
Susan Marshall Donna Thomson
Pamela Martin Pam Young
Colin McCance

SENIOR EDITOR Robin Rivers

EDITORS

Brian Cross Ann Martin
Anne Louise Mahoney Mayta Tannenbaum

PUBLICATION ADMINISTRATOR Anna Good

ART AND DESIGN

Richard Comely Ronald Migliore
Robert B. Curry Penelope Moir
George Elliott Marion Stuck
Marilyn James Bill Suddick
Robert Johanssen Sue Wilkinson

Canadian Cataloguing in Publication Data

Main entry under title:

Questions kids ask about art and entertainment

(Questions kids ask ; 10)
ISBN 0-7172-2549-6

1. Arts—Miscellanea—Juvenile literature.
2. Performing arts—Miscellanea—Juvenile literature.
3. Amusements—Miscellanea—Juvenile literature.
4. Children's questions and answers.
I. Smyth, Jocelyn.   II. Comely, Richard.   III. Series.

NX633.Q47 1988   j700'.2   C89-093162-3

Questions Kids Ask . . . about ART and ENTERTAINMENT

continued

What are the fine arts?

If you sing, play a musical instrument, take ballet lessons, paint pictures or write stories, then you are involved in the fine arts. The fine arts include painting, architecture, literature, sculpture, music and dance. Except for architecture, these things are considered more beautiful than useful. We say that they have aesthetic value. This means they are pleasing to the senses, especially sight, hearing and touch.

In the Middle Ages, there were seven fine arts: grammar, dialectic, rhetoric, arithmetic, geometry, music and astronomy. Today we consider most of these to be more related to science then art.

How is damaged art restored?

Restoring damaged art is a long, difficult process. Restoration means to make something look as it did when it was first made by repairing or retouching it.

Recently Michelangelo's paintings on the ceiling of the Sistine Chapel were restored. The scientists and artists in charge of the restoration first studied the ceiling's physical damage. Then they took photographs and divided the ceiling into sections to be studied more closely. Next, the ceiling was cleaned with special non-damaging chemicals. Again the ceiling was studied.

Cracks were filled and repaired sections were painted to complete the scene. Re-touching the painting was an extremely delicate task. First the color had to be matched exactly and then cross-hatching was added to show that it was not painted by the original artist.

Art restoration which takes into account the original artist's work is fairly new and still developing today.

How is paint made?

If you wanted to paint a picture, what do you think you would need to made your own paint? Well, you should head to the kitchen and the backyard. An egg yolk from the refrigerator and some soil or plants from the garden will give you an egg-tempera paint. Add sesame or linseed oil to dirt or plants for an oil paint. All paint—no matter if it's for painting a house or a picture—is made out of two basic ingredients: pigment and binder. The pigment, or color, is usually powdered, while the binder is a sticky liquid that holds the pigment in place and makes it easier to apply.

Many painters still use natural materials and mix them themselves, just like prehistoric people did for their cave paintings. Chalk, soil, charcoal and vegetables dyes may be used as pigments, and oil, tree resin, melted beeswax and egg yolks and whites may be used as binders. Other artists prefer to buy pre-mixed paint made from natural or artificial materials in tubes, jars or cans.

DID YOU KNOW . . . some paintbrushes are made of hog bristles!

7

What is a tutu?

Have you ever been to a ballet performance? Did you see the ballerinas wearing those frilly skirts that stick straight out?

They are called tutus, and so are the longer light, lacy skirts that end below the knee. Ballet dancers of the 16th century wore skirts which came down to the floor. These costumes were awkward and bulky. As dancers improved their skills they wanted lighter, shorter skirts which would not interfere with their body movements and would show their steps.

During the 1700s ballet costumes began to change. The skirts became shorter and shorter. Today, ballerinas wear many different costumes but the tutu is the kind of ballet skirt most often worn.

DID YOU KNOW . . . ballet historians consider a work called *Ballet Comique de la Reine* (The Queen's Comic Ballet) to be the first real ballet. Performed in Paris over 400 years ago on the occasion of a royal wedding, it lasted 5-1/2 hours!

What is an opera?

An opera is a drama set to music in which the characters sing, rather than speak, all or most of their lines. Opera involves acting, singing, costumes, scenery, music, and often dancing.

Most operas require a large cast of performers, an orchestra and complicated staging. This is why they are usually performed in specially designed theaters called opera houses. The performers are skilled musicians, known for their ability to portray a great deal of emotion in their voice. This is important because many operas deal with highly emotional themes. But not all operas are serious. Some of the most popular ones deal with funny situations. These are called ''opera buffa,'' or comic operas. The first operas were composed and performed in Italy in the 1590s. They started as a form of entertainment for the wealthy and later become popular among all types of people.

How are cartoons made?

Saturday mornings wouldn't be the same without cartoons on television. Cartoons are a kind of film technique called animation. When you watch a cartoon, you're actually watching thousands of separate still pictures flashing across the screen one after the other. Each picture is slightly different from the last, and when you see them flashing quickly, it looks like the drawings are moving.

Making cartoons is no laughing matter. It involves a lot of hard work by many talented people. The first step is to write the story, called a storyboard. Then the music and dialogue, or words, are recorded. Now layout artists, background artists and the animators who draw the characters get to work. When all of the drawings are completed they're traced onto sheets of transparent celluloid called *cels*. After the cels are painted, each one is photographed individually with a special camera. Finally the sound track is added. When everything is completed, there's your cartoon. You can certainly say that there's a lot more to cartoons than meets the eye!

What is haiku verse?

Whenever you see or sense something that is worth remembering, you can make up a very short word picture of it. If you capture that moment by writing just three short lines that don't rhyme, you will have written a haiku verse.

Haiku is a Japanese form of poetry that is hundreds of years old. Here's one of Japan's best-known haiku, written in 1686 by Matsuo Basho, a haiku master:

> *old pond*
> *a frog leaps in*
> *water's sound.*

It sounds simple, but haiku is an art that requires a great deal of skill with words and images. Originally haiku verse contained five syllables in the first line, seven in the second and five in the third. And classical Japanese haiku usually referred to one of the seasons. But over the years, the rules of haiku have become less strict. Today people all over the world write haiku in many different languages and use many different approaches. The one rule that remains is limiting haiku to three lines.

How does a drum make sound?

A drum is a percussion instrument, which means that it must be hit or struck to produce sound. Drums are made from hollow cylinders called drum shells over which a skin called a drumhead is tightly stretched. When you hit the drumhead with your hands or with drumsticks, the sound waves vibrate in the drum shell and echo off its sides, making the sound grow louder.

Try hitting the top of a table. The sound is flat and dull, isn't it? Now try hitting the side of an empty tin garbage can with a lid on it. Can you hear the difference? This sound is loud and full. Sound waves are vibrating inside the can, producing this loud, full sound. This is exactly what happens when a drummer hits a drum.

14

Why does a conductor wave a baton?

Have you ever watched an orchestra perform? Did you see a person standing in front of the orchestra waving a stick? That person is called the conductor and the stick is called a baton. The conductor uses it to guide the musicians in playing their instruments. When and how the conductor moves the baton tells them when to start playing, how quickly or slowly they must play, and whether the music should be loud or soft. When the musicians watch the conductor and the baton, they can play at the same speed and at the right volume.

In order to lead an orchestra, the conductor must know the different music for each instrument and how the orchestra should sound with everyone playing together. Conducting an orchestra is a very difficult job.

Why would they fire a cannon in a concert hall?

The Russian composer Tchaikovsky included a very different instrument in his *1812 Overture*—a cannon! The score calls for it to be blasted 16 times, one right after the other.

The *1812 Overture* was first performed in 1882, in Moscow. You could say that that was the first time a symphony audience had a real blast!

15

Where was the first circus?

Circus is a Latin word that means circle or ring. In the ancient Roman ring you could see chariot races, wrestling and witch doctors.

The circus most like our own started in 1770 in England. A man named Philip Astley opened a riding school, but soon got bored teaching his students the basic skills of horsemanship. To make things more interesting, he began to teach wire-walking, acrobatics and tricks with trained dogs. These, combined with a few clowns and some wild animals, are all the elements of our circus—which can be one of the most exciting spectacles in the world.

What is a mime?

A mime is a performer who tells stories without saying a single word! The art of acting without speaking is called pantomime. How does a mime act without speaking? By using body movements and facial expressions, the mime tells a story through gestures instead of spoken words. The word pantomime comes from a Greek word meaning "all mimic" and that is just what a mime does —mimics or imitates how people act and react without speaking.

DID YOU KNOW . . . the famous mime Marcel Marceau was the only actor to say a word in the movie called *Silent Movie.*

How do puppets work?

Do you remember the story of Pinocchio, the puppet who wanted to walk without strings? In fairytales that can happen, but in real life puppets can only be moved by a person. Puppeteers—people who work with puppets—use strings, wires, rods or their hands to control the puppets. They usually hide behind a curtain or screen so that the puppets look as if they are moving all by themselves.

Hand puppets are the most common kind. The puppeteer places the puppet over one hand and puts his or her fingers in the head and arm spaces. When the puppeteer talks, it looks as though the puppet is speaking.

Marionettes are puppets that have strings or wires that run from parts of their bodies to a frame. The puppeteer moves the frame, pulling the strings to make the puppet move.

Rod puppets have rods or sticks attached to their bodies. The puppeteer hides below the stage and moves the sticks to control the puppet.

19

Who plays a player piano?

Have you ever seen a piano playing a tune all by itself? The keys were moving up and down but no one was pushing them! You may have thought a ghost was playing, but in reality the piano has been specially designed to work without a pianist. It is called a player piano.

When you press down the key of a regular piano, a hammer inside hits a string and makes a note sound. Player pianos have a different way of making music. Inside a player piano is a roll of paper with a pattern of holes cut out of it. The holes match the notes of a piece of music. The roll of paper is pulled over a long tube, which has a row of holes along its side. The tube is connected by pipes to the hammers in the piano. When the roll of paper turns, the holes on the paper pass over the holes on the tube. Air flows into the tube and goes down the pipes. The air pushes the hammer of the note on the piano that matches the hole cut out of the paper.

What are violin strings made of?

The music from a violin is made by four strings, which are played with a bow. If you look at the strings up close, you will see that each one is different. The first string is usually made of steel. The second and third strings are made from "catgut," which does not come from a cat at all; it is made from the intestines of sheep! The fourth string is also made of catgut, and is usually covered with silver or copper wire.

DID YOU KNOW . . . a violin bow contains more than 150 horsehairs. When the bow is drawn across the violin strings the rough horsehairs make the strings vibrate, which produces the sound you hear.

Who was Houdini?

Harry Houdini was one of America's greatest magicians. Houdini became world famous in the early 1900s as an escape artist. There wasn't much he couldn't escape from, including leg irons, ten pairs of handcuffs, locked jail cells, nailed crates, and strait jackets.

Houdini, born Ehrich Weiss in Hungary in 1874, moved to Wisconsin with his family when he was a child. He took his stage name from Jean Eugène Robert-Houdin, a famous French magician of the 1800s. One of Houdini's greatest escape acts was known as the

DID YOU KNOW . . . as well as being a magician, Houdini also became an aviator and made the first flight in Australia in 1910.

Chinese Water Torture Cell. He freed himself from an airtight tank filled with water—while hanging upside down! Houdini escaped in a few seconds. (Don't try this at home!)

Where do magicians get their tricks?

You've probably seen a magician perform magic tricks. Perhaps the magician made balls appear from nowhere, pulled a rabbit out of a hat, or even made an elephant disappear. Magicians are a lot of fun to watch because they can do things no one else can.

It takes years of practice to become a good magician. This is why many of the best ones invent their own tricks, and no one but themselves knows how the trick is done. They practice the trick over and over before performing it in front of an audience. One trick can sometimes take years to get right!

If you want to practice magic on your own, ask your librarian to show you a book on magic. Many cities also have magic clubs you can join.

When were the first children's books written?

Before 1700, most books for children were not written to entertain—they taught proper behavior and school subjects. Then *Stories and Tales of Long Ago with Morals; Tales of Mother Goose,* a book of eight fairytales, appeared in English in 1729. Later editions also included rhymes and songs. *A Little Pretty Pocket-Book,* published in 1744, was filled with fables, games, rhymes and songs. The first children's novel, *The History of Little Goody Two-Shoes,* came out in 1765. Since then, children's literature has developed as a separate branch of literature.

What is a limerick?

A limerick is a popular form of light verse used in many children's rhymes. How can you tell a limerick from other types of verse? Most are five lines long and they have a certain way of rhyming. The first two lines rhyme with each other and so do the next two, and the last line rhymes with the first two lines. A good example is the famous limerick:

There was a young lady from Niger,
Who smiled as she rode on a tiger.
They came back from the ride
With the lady inside,
And the smile on the face of the tiger.

Which composer became deaf and still wrote music?

Can you imagine how hard it would be for a composer to lose all hearing? In 1798, the 28-year-old German composer Ludwig von Beethoven discovered that he was going deaf. As his deafness progressed, he became very withdrawn and went for long periods without talking to anyone. By 1820 he was almost completely deaf. Beethoven had written eight of his nine symphonies by this time. His Symphony No. 9, called the Choral Symphony, was completed after his hearing was gone. When it was performed for the first time, Beethoven could only imagine what it sounded like.

DID YOU KNOW . . . Beethoven's music is performed more often than that of any other composer.

What is jazz?

Somewhere in the United States in the 1900s a new kind of music was born—jazz. The difference between jazz and other music was that the musicians didn't memorize specific notes. Instead they improvised, or played variations of the melody. Jazz combined the rhythms of African music with the vocals of gospel and blues music. Jazz bands usually contained a trumpet, clarinet, trombone and drums or a string bass. A piano, guitar or banjo completed the band. Saxophones were added later.

Jazz became really popular in United States in the 1920s—"the golden age" of jazz. Many other kinds of music grew out of it—ragtime, blues, swing, boogie-woogie, bop, and cool jazz.

DID YOU KNOW . . . the saxophone was patented in 1846 by Adolphe Sax. It is a combination of a clarinet, an oboe and brass instruments.

27

Who walked the first tightrope?

Many centuries ago, performers called rope dancers were walking and dancing across thick ropes stretched between two poles. There are even reports, from the first century A.D., of elephants walking on ropes!

By the 16th century, rope dancing was the most popular form of circus-type entertainment. Into the 18th century, there were more rope dancers featured at fairs than any other type of performer. One famous dancer danced on the rope in boots and spurs with two children hanging from his feet. Another danced on a board 20 centimetres (8 inches) wide that was balanced on the rope. While still another would do a backward somersault from a rope 2 metres (7 feet) above the stage.

In 1750, the art of rope dancing was changed forever when a Turkish performer named Mahommed Caratha strung a wire in place of a rope and juggled ten balls while dancing across it. Most people can't even juggle ten balls!

DID YOU KNOW . . . another name for a tightrope walker is a funambulist.

Does each clown have a different face?

Each circus clown does indeed have a different face! Clowns even register their designs with the government and have them copyrighted. This means that no other clown may use the same design. It also allows clowns to pass on their designs to their children or even to sell them.

Who was the "daring young man on a flying trapeze"?

Unfortunately, one of the bravest and most inventive circus performers ever is now better remembered for the clothing he wore during his act than for the act itself. He was a Frenchman named Jules Léotard, who originated an exciting new trapeze act in the 19th century. A new art of *flying* was born in the circus.

Billed as the ''daring young man on a flying trapeze,'' Léotard performed amazing swings, swirls and somersaults in the air. The flying trapeze became the craze of the circus world. As other aerialists went on to perform even more dazzling feats, Léotard was virtually forgotten—except as the popularizer of the tight-fitting garment that now bears his name—and that was considered at the time almost as daring as his acrobatics.

What was the first comic strip?

The first comic strip to really catch on was cartoonist Richard Outcault's "Hogan's Alley." The strip starred a mischievous little creature known as the Yellow Kid. It appeared weekly in the *New York World* newspaper, starting in 1895. Because it was so popular, other newspapers soon began to run comic strips as well.

The first successful daily comic strip began to run in the *San Francisco Chronicle* in 1907. It was Bud Fisher's "Mutt and Jeff."

Since then, hundreds of comic strips have come and gone, and a few have come and stayed. Several comic strips created in the 1930s are still popular today. Chester Gould created "Dick Tracy" in 1931. And Superman also started as a comic strip in the 30s, created by Jerry Siegel and Joe Shuster.

Who are Punch and Judy?

For over 300 years, a bad-tempered, brawling hand puppet named Punch has been making audiences laugh. Punch and his quarrelsome wife Judy became famous puppet characters in England in the 1660s.

Punch is a hunchback with a hooked nose and chin, and a fat belly. He not only fights with his wife, but also battles with a doctor, a hangman and even a crocodile. And Punch is always the winner.

Index